May God always bless you!

Christmas 2017

## This book belongs to:

Dylan Watson

Love you more than bacteria Little Pops!

Love Always,

Dad

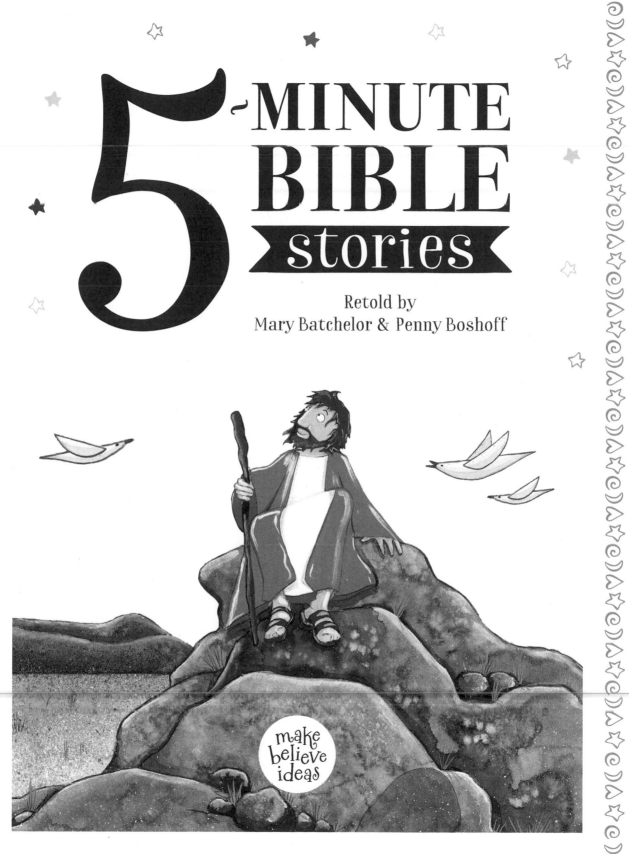

# 5-MINUTE BIBLE stories

Retold by
Mary Batchelor & Penny Boshoff

make believe ideas

Copyright © 2017

**make believe ideas ltd**

The Wilderness, Berkhamsted, Hertfordshire, HP4 2AZ, UK.
501 Nelson Place, P.O. Box 141000, Nashville, TN 37214-1000, USA.

Retold by Mary Batchelor and Penny Boshoff.
Some of the material contained in this book previously
appeared in *My First Bedtime Bible* © 2005 make believe ideas ltd,
and *My First Read-Aloud Bible* © 2009 make believe ideas ltd.

Illustrated by Sara Baker and Nikki Loy.
Additional illustrations by Jo Goodberry,
Helen Parrott, and Cathy Shimmen.

ISBN: 978-1-786-92781-1

# Contents

# Old Testament Stories

# Making our world

Long ago, when God began
to make everything, the earth
was dark and empty.

God said, "Earth needs light."
And light appeared.
God made the sun to shine by
day and the moon and stars
to light the night.

God was pleased with
what he had done.

DEAR GOD, THANK YOU FOR MAKING
OUR BEAUTIFUL WORLD. AMEN.

# God fills the world

God said, "I will make grass and flowers and trees to cover Earth."

Then he made all kinds of creatures.
He made fish to swim in the rivers
and seas. Birds and butterflies to fill the air.
And animals, big and small, to play on the land.

What sorts of big and small animals live near you?

THANK YOU, GOD, FOR ALL THE DIFFERENT BIRDS AND ANIMALS AND FOR THE SOUNDS THEY MAKE. AMEN.

# Adam and Eve

God wanted someone to love. So he made Adam and Eve to be his friends and to take care of his Earth.

What plants and animals can you see in the garden?

"Enjoy the fruit in my garden," said God. Then he pointed to one tree. "But don't eat fruit from that tree. If you do, you will die."

Adam and Eve were very happy in God's garden.

THANK YOU, GOD, FOR MAKING PEOPLE
AND FOR MAKING ME. AMEN.

# Forbidden fruit

The fruit on the forbidden tree looked delicious. "Why not try it?" the snake asked. "But God said we would die," said Eve.

"Don't listen to God," the snake whispered.

DEAR GOD, I'M SORRY FOR SOMETIMES BEING DISOBEDIENT. PLEASE FORGIVE ME. AMEN.

Why do you think Adam and Eve ate the fruit?

So Eve picked some and shared it with Adam.

God was sad that they had disobeyed him.

Now Adam and Eve had to leave God's garden.

# Cain and Abel

Adam and Eve had two sons: Cain and Abel.
Cain thought that God loved Abel more than him.
So he hated his brother more and more.

One day when they were out in the fields, Cain killed Abel.

God was very sad. Hate and murder were spoiling his Earth. Cain had to leave home and move far away.

DEAR GOD, HELP ME NOT TO BE JEALOUS OF OTHER CHILDREN. AMEN.

# Noah and the flood

Nobody on Earth listened to God—except Noah.
"Noah, there's going to be a flood," said God.
"Build a big boat for your family. And take two
of every kind of animal and bird with you."

PLEASE, GOD, KEEP US SAFE, TOO.
AMEN.

Noah did what God told him. Then it rained and rained. Water covered the land. But Noah's boat floated safely.

# Rainbow in the sky

At last the rain stopped. When the land was dry, Noah opened the door.

Out flew the birds.
Off scampered the animals.
And Noah said a special
thank-you to God.

"Noah," said God, "when you see the rainbow, remember my promise: I will never flood the whole earth again."

Have you ever seen a rainbow after it has rained?

THANK YOU, GOD, FOR THE BEAUTIFUL COLORS OF THE RAINBOW. AMEN.

# God chooses Abraham

Abraham and Sarah longed for a baby.
One day God said, "Abraham, I've chosen you.
"So leave your house and take your tent.
We're going on a journey."

Why do you think God chose Abraham? What sort of person do you think he was?

THANK YOU, DEAR GOD, THAT WE ARE
ALL SPECIAL TO YOU. AMEN.

"I will give you a new land and a big family.
Everyone in the whole world will be happy
because of you and your family."

# Three strangers

One hot day Abraham saw three tired strangers.
"Come and rest here!" he called.

THANK YOU, GOD, FOR MOTHERS
AND GRANDMAS. AMEN.

Do you think God was pleased that Abraham offered the strangers food and rest? Why?

So they sat in the shade while Abraham brought them food and water. He didn't guess that they were God's messengers. "Next year Sarah will have a baby boy," they said.

# Isaac

God kept his promise and baby Isaac was born.

HELP ME, GOD, TO TRUST YOU ALWAYS,
NO MATTER WHAT. AMEN.

Some years later, God said, "Abraham, will you give Isaac back to me?"

How did God find out that Abraham truly trusted him?

But just as Abraham was getting ready to give Isaac back, God called out, "Abraham, I know now how much you love and trust me. I won't take Isaac away."

# Esau and Jacob

Isaac married Rebekah and they had twin sons: Esau and Jacob.

Do you think this was a fair swap? Why?

One day Esau arrived back from hunting. Jacob was cooking delicious food.

28

"Give me some!" cried Esau. "I'm starving!"
"Only if you give me your special place
as eldest son," said Jacob.

"All right!" Esau agreed.

DEAR GOD, HELP ME TO BE FAIR
TO OTHERS. AMEN.

# Jacob's dream

Jacob tricked Esau again. Esau wanted to kill Jacob. So Jacob ran away.

That night Jacob slept under the stars.

THANK YOU, GOD, FOR BEING WITH US ALL NIGHT LONG. AMEN.

In his dream he
saw a staircase.
Angels were going
up and down.

Where do you
think the staircase
might lead to?

Then God said, "Jacob, I promise to be with you.
I'll never leave you. You and your family will
have the good things I promised to Abraham."

# Joseph's coat

Jacob had lots of children but Joseph was his favorite. He gave Joseph a beautiful coat. Joseph's brothers were jealous.

HELP ME, DEAR GOD,
TO ALWAYS BE KIND. AMEN.

One day Joseph went to the fields to find his brothers.

How would you feel if someone was given a special coat, but not you?

"Let's get him," the brothers cried. They grabbed Joseph, ripped off his special coat, and threw him down an empty well.

# Joseph goes to Egypt

The brothers decided to sell Joseph to some men traveling to Egypt.

In Egypt, Joseph became Potiphar's slave.

Because Joseph worked so hard, Potiphar put him in charge of everything he had.

But Potiphar's wife told lies about Joseph, so he was sent to prison. Even there, God was still with him.

Who was mean to Joseph, and who was kind to him?

HELP ME, DEAR GOD, NOT TO TELL LIES ABOUT OTHER CHILDREN. AMEN.

# Joseph saves Egypt

The king of Egypt had worrying dreams. "Fetch Joseph," a servant said. "He understands dreams."

The king told Joseph his dream. "God says seven good harvests are coming, followed by seven bad ones," Joseph explained. "Save food now to feed your people in the bad years."

The king was pleased. "Joseph, you must help me lead Egypt."

# Brothers reunited

Now Joseph's brothers had to travel to Egypt to buy corn. They did not know that the man in charge was Joseph. Joseph pretended to be angry.

DEAR GOD, HELP ME TO BE
FORGIVING LIKE JOSEPH. AMEN.

Then he said, "Don't be frightened. It's me, Joseph! I will take care of you. God brought me here to save everyone! Come and live in Egypt."

Had Joseph forgiven his brothers? How can you tell?

# Moses

God gave Jacob the name "Israel." Israel's people stayed in Egypt. But years later, a cruel king made them his slaves.

"Kill all their baby boys!" he ordered. But one mother hid her baby in a floating basket among the river reeds.

"What's in that basket?" asked the princess.
Her servant opened the lid.

"What a beautiful baby!" the princess exclaimed.
"I shall keep him and name him Moses."

How did baby Moses survive?

PLEASE, GOD, TAKE CARE OF BABIES.
AMEN.

# Fire in the bush

When Moses grew up he longed to save his people. The king was furious, so Moses ran far away.

One day, Moses saw a bush on fire. "That's strange!" he thought.

Suddenly God spoke from the bush.
"Moses, go back to Egypt and
rescue your unhappy people."

Why do you think
Moses said
"I can't!" to God?

"I can't!" Moses exclaimed.
"Yes, you can," God said, "because I will be with you."

THANK YOU, DEAR GOD, FOR ALWAYS
BEING WITH US. AMEN.

# Moses warns the king

Moses set off for Egypt.
"God says you must let his
people go," he told the king.

Do you think
Moses was brave
to stand up to
the king?

PLEASE HELP ME, GOD, TO BE OBEDIENT.
AMEN.

"NO!" the king replied. "I don't know or care about your God. I won't let them go. Make the Israelites work harder!"

"Obey God or bad things will happen," Moses warned. "I won't!" the king replied.

# Chaos in Egypt

Everything happened as Moses had warned. First frogs ran everywhere, then flies came, then there were storms.

But still the king would not let the Israelites go.

THANK YOU, GOD, FOR KEEPING YOUR PEOPLE SAFE. AMEN.

"God will rescue his people," Moses said, "but because of you, Egypt will be sad."

"Go away!" the king shouted.

Should the king have listened to Moses? Why?

"Tomorrow God will rescue us," Moses told the Israelites. "Cook a special meal to thank him."

# The waves roll back

The next day the Israelites left Egypt and camped by the Red Sea. But the Egyptian army chased them!

God said, "Moses, stretch your stick over the sea. Tell the people to go forward."

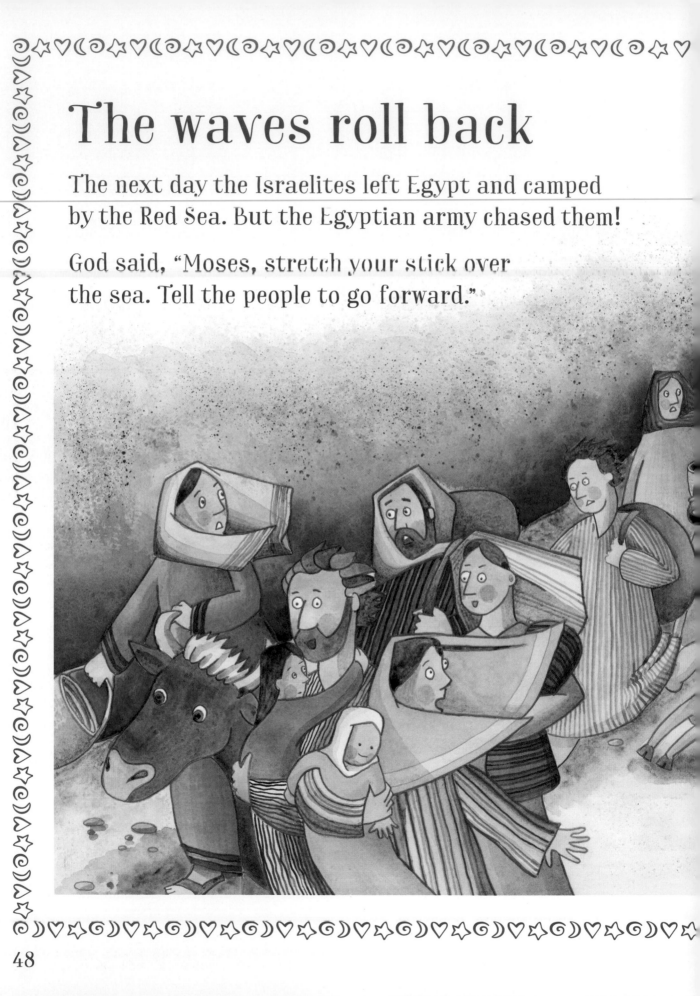

Moses obeyed God. The waters rolled back and the Israelites crossed on dry ground.

"Hurrah!" they shouted on the other side. "God has rescued us!"

How did the Israelites get to the other side of the Red Sea?

DEAR GOD, THANK YOU FOR RESCUING THE ISRAELITES. AMEN.

# God sends food

"God is leading us to the country he promised us," Moses told the Israelites as they walked through the desert.

"There's nothing to eat!" the people grumbled.
"I will feed you every day," God promised.

The next morning the ground was
covered with small white flakes.
They tasted good, like honey biscuits.

Why weren't the Israelites happy to be free at first?

THANK YOU, GOD, FOR OUR FOOD EACH DAY.
AMEN.

# God gives water

The people kept grumbling. "We're thirsty, Moses," they moaned. "Give us water!"

Moses told God and God said, "Go to the special rock that I will show you and hit it with your stick."

THANK YOU, DEAR GOD, FOR CLEAN WATER. AMEN.

Moses did as God told him and cool, refreshing water gushed from the rock. There was plenty for everyone.

How did the Israelites get food and water in the desert?

# Rules for the people

God said to Moses, "These rules will help my people every day: Put me first and love me best. Don't worship anyone but me. Don't use my name carelessly. Keep one day each week as a resting day with me.

"Obey your father and mother. Don't hurt others. Keep love between a husband and wife special. Don't take what isn't yours. Don't tell lies about other people. Don't be jealous of other people and want what they have."

Do you think these rules are still important today? Why?

PLEASE, GOD, HELP ME TO DO WHAT MY PARENTS TELL ME. AMEN.

# Reaching Canaan

When they reached the land God had promised them, Moses sent twelve spies to look around.

Do you think the people believed God would help them win the land?

"It's a wonderful country," the spies said, "but we'll never win it! The people there are huge and strong!" But Caleb and Joshua shouted out, "God will help us!" And He did.

DEAR GOD, HELP ME WHEN I DON'T KNOW WHAT TO DO. AMEN.

# Samson's riddle

Enemies attacked Israel and God chose strong Samson to fight them.

Samson told his enemies this riddle:
"Out of the eater came something to eat.
Out of the strong came something sweet."

DEAR GOD, THANK YOU FOR
THE FOOD WE EAT. AMEN.

His enemies, the Philistines, were puzzled. Then they discovered that Samson had found a bee's nest in a lion's dead body and he'd eaten the delicious honey.

What was the eater? What was the thing it ate?

# Samson and the Philistines

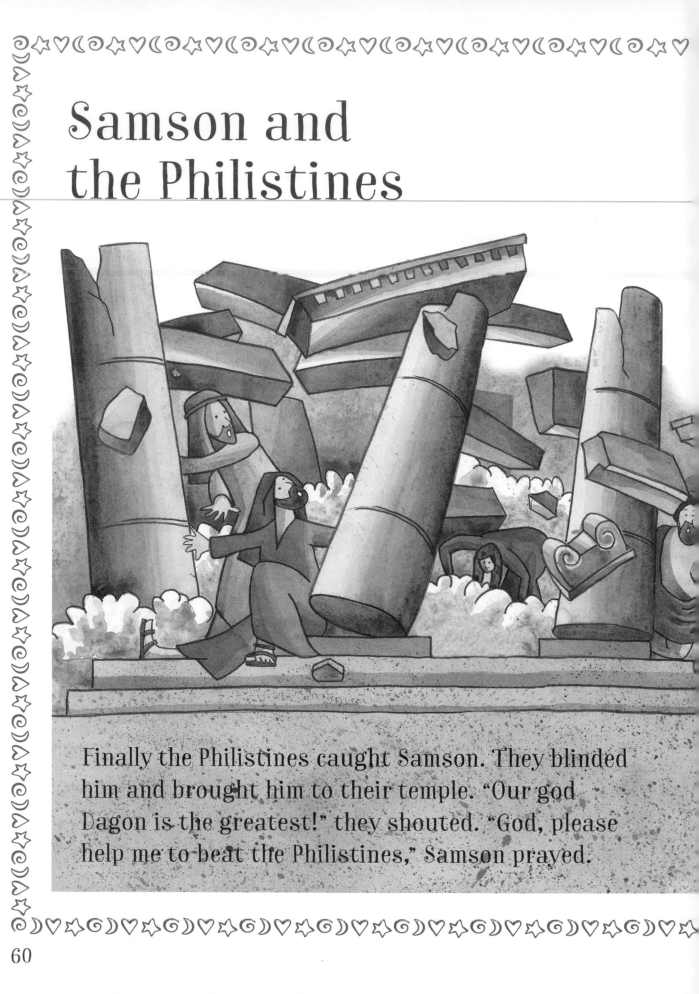

Finally the Philistines caught Samson. They blinded him and brought him to their temple. "Our god Dagon is the greatest!" they shouted. "God, please help me to beat the Philistines," Samson prayed.

He put his hands on the big pillars and pushed and pushed. Crack. CRASH! The temple fell down and killed everyone. Samson was remembered as a great hero.

# Naomi and Ruth

Naomi's family lived in Bethlehem. But when the food ran out, they moved to far-away Moab.

Poor Naomi! Her husband and sons died. But their Moabite wives, Orpah and Ruth, looked after her.

THANK YOU, GOD, FOR EVERYONE WHO TAKES CARE OF ME. AMEN.

Do you think it would have been hard for Ruth to move countries?

"I'm going back to Bethlehem," Naomi said.
"Good-bye," said Orpah, hugging Naomi.

But Ruth said, "I'm coming with you. I'll stay with you always. I love you and your God will be my God."

# A happy ending

Naomi and Ruth arrived in Bethlehem. They were so poor that Ruth picked up leftover grain from the fields to make bread.

"Who's that stranger?" asked the farmer Boaz.

DEAR GOD, THANK YOU FOR MY LOVING FAMILY. AMEN.

"That's Ruth. She takes good care of Naomi," the farmworkers replied.
"Then drop extra grain for Ruth," Boaz said kindly.
Boaz decided to marry Ruth.

Why do you think Boaz wanted to marry Ruth?

They soon had a little boy. Now Naomi was very happy.

# God answers a prayer

Hannah longed for a baby!
One day, she visited God's
house with her husband.
Hannah felt so sad.

"Please God," she cried, "send me a baby. I promise I'll give him back to you."

Eli, the priest, heard her. "May God answer your prayer!" he said. And God did!

Do you think the priest was a good man? Why?

Hannah called her baby Samuel.

THANK YOU, GOD, FOR LISTENING WHEN WE FEEL SAD. AMEN.

# God calls Samuel

Hannah kept her promise.
She took Samuel to live with Eli,
the priest, at God's house.

One night, Samuel heard a voice:
"Samuel!"
He ran to Eli.
"I didn't call," Eli said.
"Go back to bed."

DEAR GOD, HELP ME TO LISTEN
WHEN YOU SPEAK TO ME. AMEN.

Three times Samuel heard the voice and three times he ran to Eli.

Then Eli said, "It's God's voice. Next time he calls, say, 'I'm listening.'"

God called again and Samuel listened to God's message.

How did Eli help Samuel?

# King of Israel

Samuel gave God's messages to the Israelites.
But they wanted a king instead.
"I will choose their king," God told Samuel.

One day a young man called Saul arrived.
"My father's donkeys ran
away," he told Samuel.

Why do you think the Israelites wanted a king?

"I can't find them anywhere. Can you help me?"

"Don't worry, your donkeys have been found," Samuel said. "God has chosen you to be king of Israel!"

PLEASE, GOD, HELP ME WHEN I'M WORRIED.
AMEN.

# Saul disobeys God

One day the Israelites were getting ready for battle.

"Wait for me to pray before you fight," Samuel told King Saul.

King Saul waited and waited. Finally, he decided to say the prayers himself. Just then Samuel came back.

When have you found it hard to wait for something?

"Why didn't you wait?" Samuel asked sadly. "Because you won't obey God, he is going to choose another king."

PLEASE, GOD, HELP ME LEARN HOW TO WAIT. AMEN.

# A new king

"Go and see Jesse," God told Samuel.
"I have chosen one of his sons to be king."

Jesse's eldest son was handsome.
"He looks like a king!" thought Samuel.
But God whispered, "No! Not this one."

Samuel saw six more sons. But each time God said, "No!"

"Have you another son?" Samuel asked.
"Only young David," Jesse replied.
"He's looking after my sheep."

When David arrived,
God told Samuel,
"He is the one!
My chosen king!"

Do you think Samuel was surprised by God's choice of king? Why?

THANK YOU, GOD, FOR LOVING US WHATEVER WE LOOK LIKE. AMEN.

# David and Goliath

David's brothers were in Saul's army. David was visiting them when the huge Philistine soldier, Goliath, bellowed, "Israelites, choose a man to fight me!"

The Israelites were terrified.

Would you have wanted to fight the giant? Why?

"I'll fight him!" said David, taking just his shepherd's sling and five stones.
"I'll feed you to the birds!" roared Goliath.
"I fight with God's strength!" David shouted.
He aimed. The stone from his sling hit Goliath's skull . . . crack! Goliath crashed to the ground.

PLEASE, GOD, HELP US TO STAND UP
FOR WHAT IS RIGHT. AMEN.

# David and Jonathan

Saul invited David to live in his palace. Whenever Saul was miserable, David would sing and play his harp to cheer him up.

David and Jonathan, Saul's son, became great friends. But Saul grew jealous of David.

THANK YOU, GOD, FOR BEST FRIENDS. AMEN.

# David becomes king

One day Saul and Jonathan died in battle and David became king.

"Jonathan is dead," David said sadly. "I must look after his family." "Then take care of his son Mephibosheth," a servant said. "He can't walk."

So David invited Jonathan's son to the palace. "Welcome, Mephibosheth," he said.

"Come and live here and have dinner with me every day."

How did David repay Jonathan's kindness?

THANK YOU, GOD, FOR KIND PEOPLE. AMEN.

# Wise Solomon

When David died, his son Solomon became king. Solomon asked God to help him rule well. God made him wise.

DEAR GOD, GIVE US WISE PARENTS AND TEACHERS. AMEN.

One day two mothers arrived with a baby.
"He's my baby!" the first woman cried.
"No! He's mine," the other shouted.
"Cut the baby in two," ordered Solomon,
"and give each mother half!"
"No!" cried the first woman.
"Don't hurt him!
Let her have him!"
"Take the baby,"
Solomon told the
first woman,
"for you are the
real mother."

How did Solomon know who the real mother was?

# A temple for God

God made Solomon rich as well as wise. Solomon began to build a splendid home for God – the temple.

Thousands of builders got busy with fine wood and huge stones. Inside, in God's special room, even the floor was paved with gold!

THANK YOU, GOD, FOR LISTENING TO US WHEREVER WE ARE. AMEN.

Finally it was finished. Everyone celebrated.
God promised to listen to his people
when they prayed to him there.

# Jonah and the big fish

God told Jonah, "Go to the people of Nineveh.
Tell them to stop being wicked." Jonah didn't
want to go. He ran away and went to sea.

HELP ME, GOD, TO DO WHAT I'M TOLD.
AMEN.

But God sent a strong wind to whip up the waves. "We're going to sink!" cried the terrified sailors.

Why did Jonah ask to be thrown in the sea?

"It's my fault!" Jonah said. "I ran away from God. Throw me in the sea, then the storm will stop." The sailors threw Jonah overboard and the sea grew calm.

# God forgives

As Jonah sank beneath the waves, a big fish swam by and swallowed him up.

Inside the fish Jonah prayed,
"Please help me, God!"
God listened. He told the fish
to spit Jonah out on the beach.

So Jonah went to Nineveh. The people listened to him. They promised to stop being wicked. "I forgive them," God told Jonah. But Jonah was angry. He did not want God to forgive his enemies.

Is it easy or hard to forgive our enemies? Why?

THANK YOU, GOD, FOR FORGIVING ME WHEN I'M TRULY SORRY. AMEN.

Is it better to obey God or a king? Why?

# Daniel

Israel's cleverest young men were taken to Nebuchadnezzar's palace. "Eat the food the king sends you," the chief servant ordered. But Daniel, Shadrach, Meshach, and Abednego knew that meant obeying the king rather than God.

PLEASE, GOD, HELP ME TO OBEY YOU.
AMEN.

"Give us vegetables and water for ten days," Daniel begged. The servant agreed. After ten days they looked fit and healthy. "These men are the best!" Nebuchadnezzar said. "They will help me rule."

# Saved from the fire

"Bow down to my wonderful gold statue!"
Nebuchadnezzar ordered. Everyone bowed down
except Shadrach, Meshach, and Abednego.

"Bow down!" Nebuchadnezzar
shouted. "Or I'll throw
you into the fire!"

Were Shadrach,
Meshach, and
Abednego brave
men? Why?

"We bow only to God!" the friends replied bravely. So Nebuchadnezzar's soldiers threw them into the flames. Suddenly Nebuchadnezzar gasped: "We threw three men in—but there are four walking about in the fire! Their God has sent his angel to keep them safe!"

THANK YOU, GOD, FOR ANGELS
WHO LOOK AFTER US. AMEN.

# Daniel and the lions

The new king liked Daniel. This made people jealous. "Order everyone to pray to you alone— or be thrown to the lions," they told the king.

"Daniel is still praying to God!" said his enemies. So the king's soldiers threw Daniel into the lions' pit.

THANK YOU, GOD, FOR
KEEPING DANIEL SAFE. AMEN.

The king lay awake worrying. The next morning, he shouted, "Daniel! Did God save you?"

Why did the king lay worrying at night?

"Yes!" Daniel replied. "My God closed the lions' mouths! I'm safe!"

# New Testament Stories

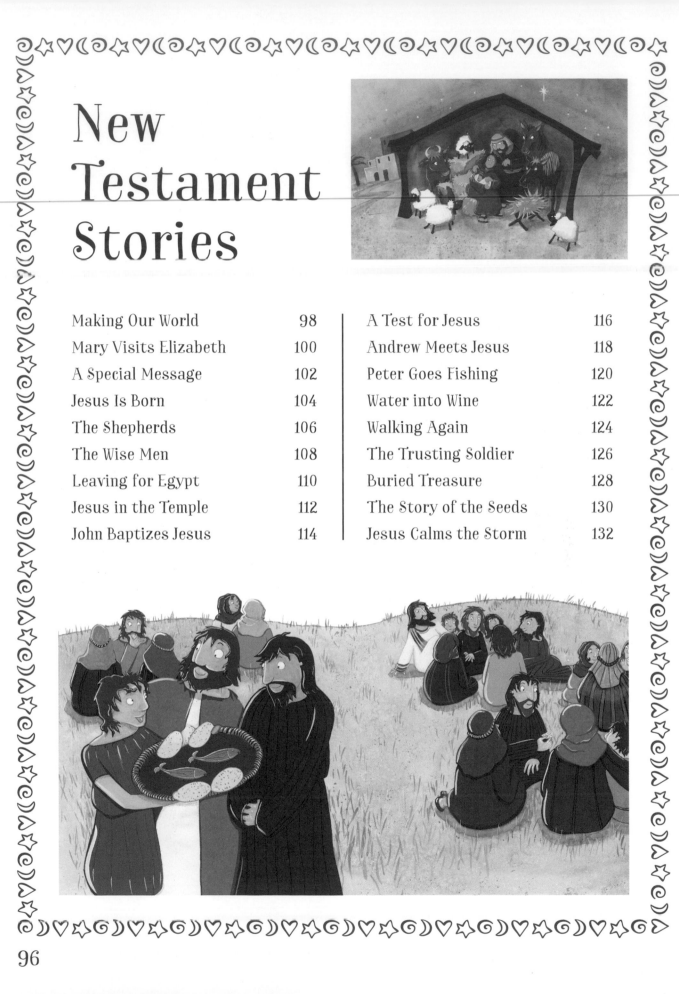

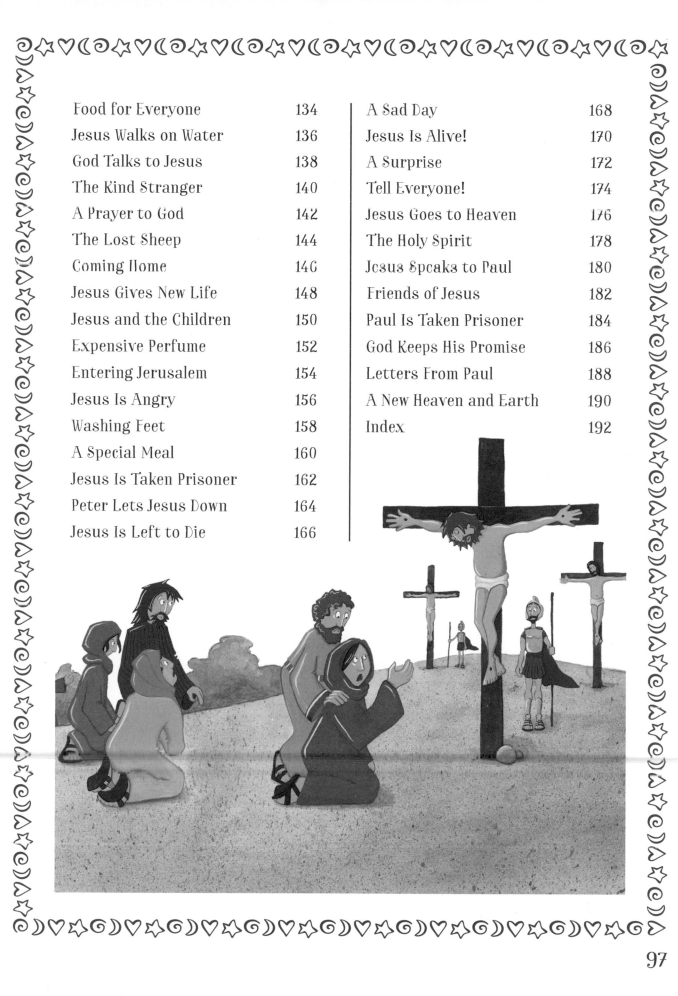

# Making our world

One day God sent the angel Gabriel to see Mary. "Mary, don't be afraid, God is pleased with you," Gabriel said. "You are going to have a baby. Call him Jesus. He will be a great king." Mary looked puzzled.

The baby will be God's Son," Gabriel explained.
"I will do whatever God wants," Mary replied.

THANK YOU, GOD, THAT MARY WAS GLAD
TO DO WHAT YOU ASKED. AMEN.

# Mary visits Elizabeth

Mary couldn't wait to tell her cousin Elizabeth the news. She left home and hurried off. "Elizabeth!" she called, running to the house.

DEAR GOD, HELP ME TO REMEMBER TO THANK YOU, JUST LIKE MARY DID. AMEN.

Elizabeth hugged her. "Mary! How wonderful! As soon as I heard you I knew that God had chosen you to be the mother of his promised king!"

What can you say thank you to God for?

Mary was so happy she sang "thank you" to God.

# A special message

Joseph wanted to marry Mary. When he heard about Mary's baby he was worried.

That night, God's angel gave Joseph a special message.

DEAR GOD, HELP ME TO BE LIKE JOSEPH AND LISTEN TO WHAT YOU SAY. AMEN.

"Joseph, don't worry!" the angel said. "God wants you to marry Mary."

Do you think Joseph was happy to get the angel's message? Why?

"Her baby has been made by God's Holy Spirit. Call him Jesus. One day he will rescue God's people." So Joseph married Mary.

# Jesus is born

Bethlehem was busy. Mary and Joseph had traveled all the way from Nazareth. They needed somewhere to sleep, but all the inns were full.

At last Joseph found somewhere warm and dry—a stable! That night, Jesus was born. Mary wrapped him up warmly and laid him to sleep in the hay.

# The shepherds

Shepherds were looking after their sheep when an angel appeared. God's dazzling light shone around.

How would you react if an angel appeared?

"Don't be afraid!" said the angel. "I have good news! God's special king has been born in Bethlehem. You will find him lying in a manger."

Suddenly, the sky was filled with angels singing to God. The shepherds ran to Bethlehem. They were so happy when they found Jesus!

DEAR GOD, THANK YOU FOR SENDING YOUR ANGELS WITH THE GOOD NEWS ABOUT JESUS. AMEN.

# The wise men

Far away in the East, some wise men saw a bright new star. "How wonderful!" they cried. "A great king has been born! Let's go and worship him!"

So they followed the star until it stopped over a house in Bethlehem.

What did the wise men think the star was a sign of?

The wise men were so happy to see Jesus. They bowed down low and gave him precious gifts—gold, frankincense, and myrrh.

THANK YOU, GOD, FOR MAKING THE STARS, ESPECIALLY THE ONE THAT LED THE WISE MEN TO JESUS. AMEN.

# Leaving for Egypt

After the wise men had gone, Joseph saw an angel in his dreams. "Joseph! Get up!" said the angel. "Hurry! Cruel King Herod wants to hurt Jesus. Go to Egypt. You will all be safe there. I will tell you when to come back."

Do you think it would have been scary escaping to Egypt?

DEAR GOD, YOU KEPT JESUS AND HIS FAMILY SAFE. PLEASE KEEP MY FAMILY SAFE, TOO. AMEN.

Joseph leaped out of bed. He woke
Mary and Jesus. They packed
their bags and left at once.

After King Herod died, an angel told
Joseph it was safe to return home.

# Jesus in the temple

Mary, Joseph, and Jesus had been worshiping God in Jerusalem. They were traveling home to Nazareth.

Why did Jesus call the temple his Father's house?

"Have you seen Jesus?" Mary asked.
Joseph shook his head. Oh no! Jesus had been
left behind. Mary and Joseph rushed back to
Jerusalem. They found Jesus in the temple.
"I've been here in my Father's house," said Jesus.

PLEASE KEEP ME BY YOUR SIDE, GOD.
AMEN.

# John baptizes Jesus

"Come back to God!" John shouted. "Say you are sorry and get baptized in the water so that God will forgive you and make you clean inside and out!"

The people did what John told them. Jesus was good. But he came to be baptized, too. He always did what God wanted.

How do people get baptized in your church?

When Jesus came out of the water, God said, "You are my own dear Son. I am pleased with you!"

DEAR GOD, I'VE DONE WRONG THINGS. I'M SORRY. I'M GLAD THAT YOU MAKE ME CLEAN INSIDE. AMEN.

# A test for Jesus

Jesus went into the desert to get ready to do God's work. God's enemy, the devil, came to trick Jesus. "I'll give you the whole world, if you bow down to me," he said.

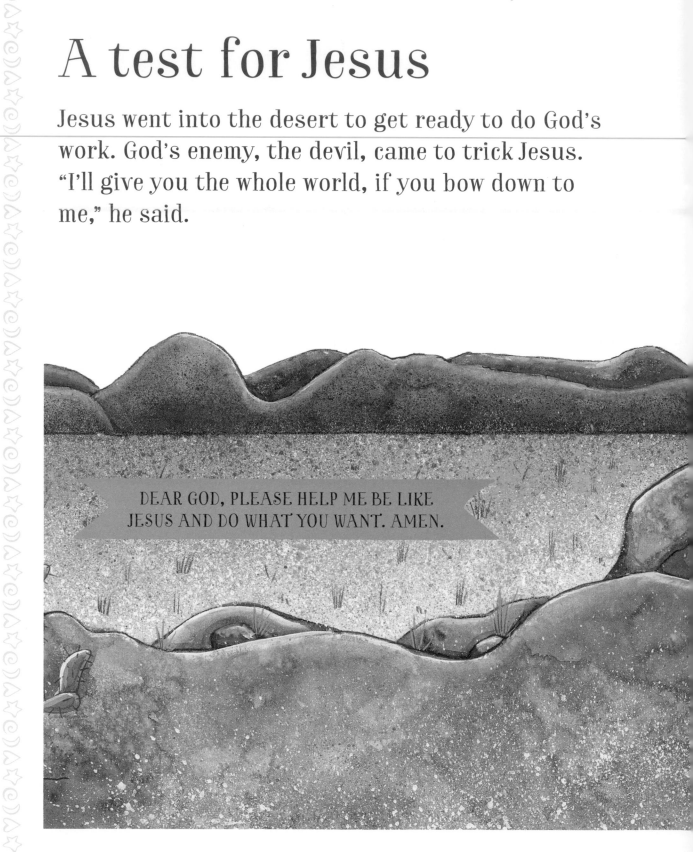

DEAR GOD, PLEASE HELP ME BE LIKE JESUS AND DO WHAT YOU WANT. AMEN.

"No!" said Jesus. "God has told everyone to bow down and serve no one else but him." Jesus chose to listen to God, not the devil, so the devil left.

Have you ever been asked to do something wrong, but not done it?

# Andrew meets Jesus

One day Andrew and his friend followed Jesus.
"Where do you live?" Andrew called out.
"Come and see!" said Jesus.

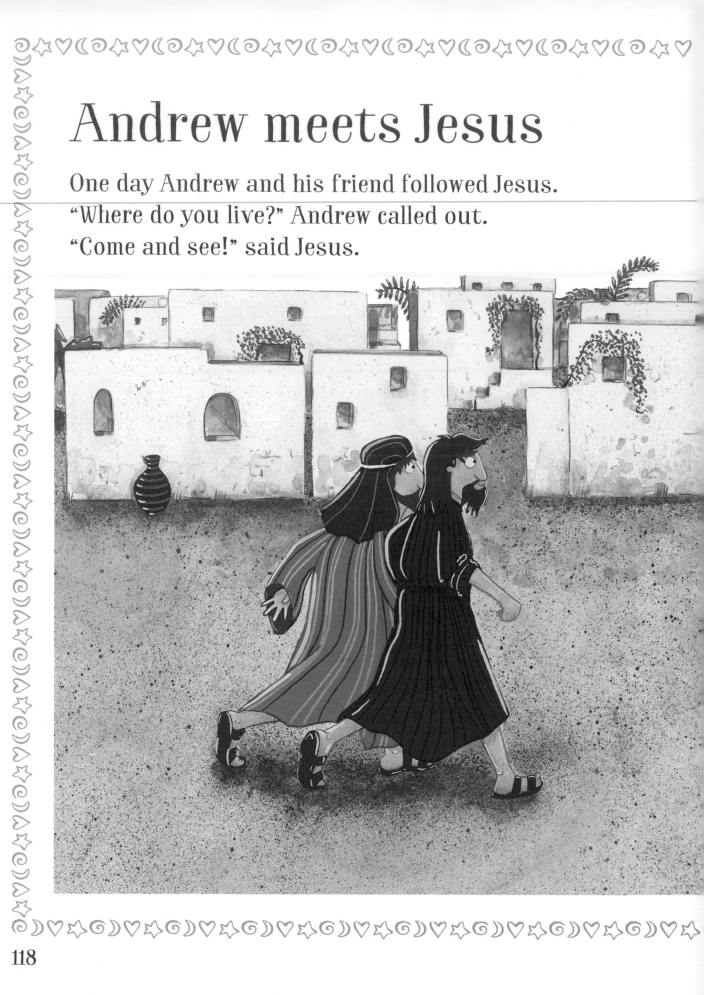

So they went to Jesus' house and talked with him all afternoon. Then Andrew rushed to find his brother. "Peter!" he said, "Come and meet Jesus, he's the king God promised us!"

Why do you think Andrew followed Jesus?

THANK YOU, DEAR GOD, FOR MY HOME. AMEN.

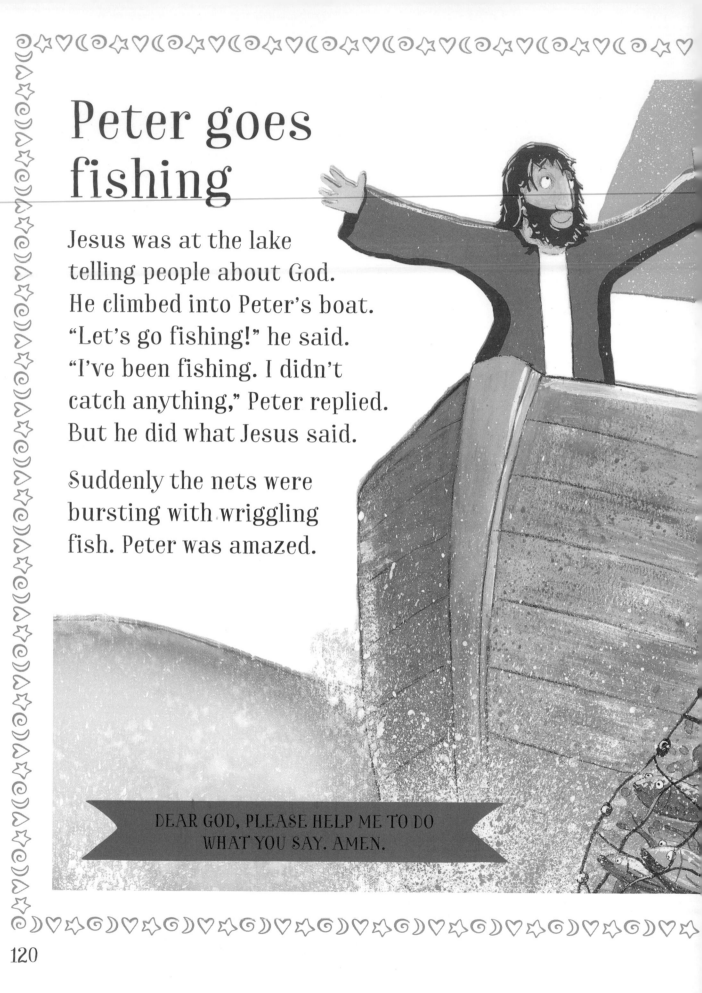

# Peter goes fishing

Jesus was at the lake telling people about God. He climbed into Peter's boat. "Let's go fishing!" he said. "I've been fishing. I didn't catch anything," Peter replied. But he did what Jesus said.

Suddenly the nets were bursting with wriggling fish. Peter was amazed.

DEAR GOD, PLEASE HELP ME TO DO WHAT YOU SAY. AMEN.

"Peter, come with me and we'll go fishing for people!" Jesus said. So Peter left his boat and followed Jesus.

Do you think Peter found it hard to leave his home and job?

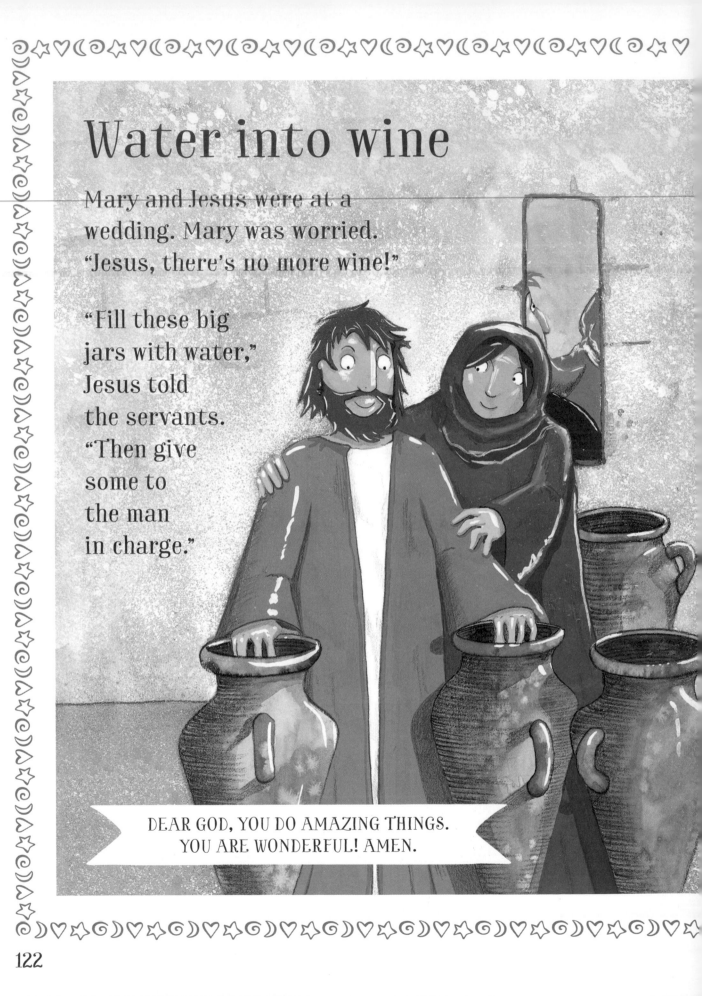

# Water into wine

Mary and Jesus were at a wedding. Mary was worried. "Jesus, there's no more wine!"

"Fill these big jars with water," Jesus told the servants. "Then give some to the man in charge."

DEAR GOD, YOU DO AMAZING THINGS. YOU ARE WONDERFUL! AMEN.

When the servants did what Jesus told them, they were amazed. Jesus had turned ordinary water into the very best wine!

Why did Mary tell Jesus that the wine had run out?

# Walking again

"Jesus will help you walk again," said the men as they carried their friend to Jesus' house.

The house was too crowded. So they cut a hole in the roof and lowered their friend down.

THANK YOU, DEAR GOD, FOR LOOKING AFTER PEOPLE WHO ARE UNWELL. AMEN.

Jesus smiled and said to the man, "I forgive you. Now get up and walk home!"

To everyone's amazement, the man stood up and began to walk!

Why were the people amazed?

# The trusting soldier

An important soldier came to Jesus.
"My servant is very ill!" he said.

DEAR GOD, THE SOLDIER TRUSTED JESUS.
HELP ME TO TRUST JESUS, TOO. AMEN.

"I'll come and make him well," said Jesus.
"You don't need to come to my house," the soldier said.
"Just give the order and my servant will get better."
"I'm pleased you trust me so much," said Jesus.
"Go home, your servant is well now."

What did Jesus like about the soldier?

# Buried treasure

"When you find God's kingdom, you will never let it go," Jesus said to his friends. And he told them this story:

A man was digging in a field when he found treasure. "If I buy this field, the treasure will be mine!" he thought.

So he sold everything he had. Then he bought the field. He was so happy— now the treasure was his forever!

The man gave up things to buy the field. What do we give up to go to heaven?

GOD, YOU ARE THE BEST TREASURE OF ALL. AMEN.

# The story of the seeds

"If you listen to me," said Jesus,
"you'll be like the good soil in this story."

A farmer sowed his seeds. Some seeds fell
on the path. The birds gobbled them up.

The seeds among the stones grew quickly, but they dried up in the hot sun.

Other seeds grew well until the weeds got in their way.

The seeds on the good soil grew into tall, healthy plants.

How are God's words like the seeds in this story?

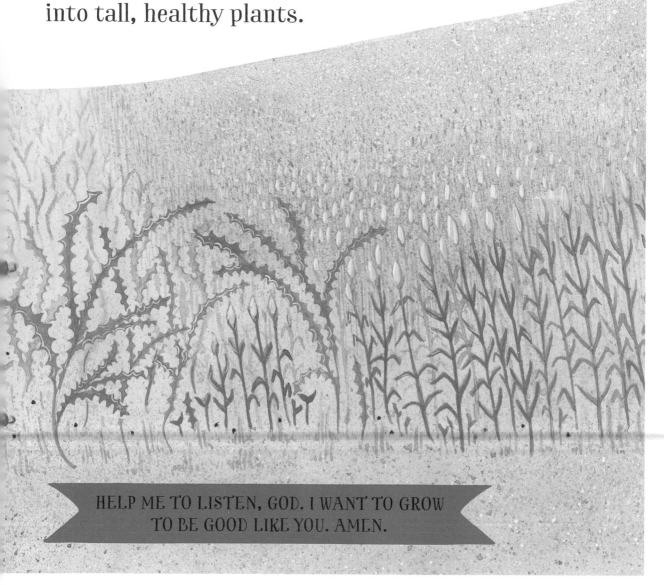

HELP ME TO LISTEN, GOD. I WANT TO GROW TO BE GOOD LIKE YOU. AMEN.

# Jesus calms the storm

It had been a busy day. Jesus was fast asleep in his friends' boat. Suddenly a wild wind whipped up the waves. They came crashing over the boat.

DEAR JESUS, THANK YOU FOR HELPING YOUR FRIENDS IN THE STORM. AMEN.

"Wake up, Jesus!" his friends shouted. "The boat is sinking!" Jesus got up. "Waves! Calm down!" he ordered. "Wind, be quiet!"

Why did Jesus' followers think this was such a big miracle?

At once all was safe and still. Jesus' friends were amazed. "Even the wind and waves do what Jesus says!"

# Food for everyone

The crowd had listened to Jesus all day.
"They're hungry," said Jesus.
"Let's give them some food."

THANK YOU, GOD, FOR ALL OUR FOOD.
AMEN.

"We don't have enough money!" his friends replied.
"This boy has five little loaves and two fish,"
said Andrew. Jesus took the loaves and
the fish and thanked God for them.

How did Jesus feed the hungry crowd?

Then he handed out the food.
And everyone had plenty to eat!

# Jesus walks on water

One evening Jesus went away to pray.
His friends set off across the lake.
They puffed and panted as they rowed.

Suddenly they saw someone walking on the water toward them. "It's a ghost!" they screamed.

"Don't be scared," said the man, climbing into their boat. "It's me, Jesus!" The friends were amazed. It was Jesus!

Why do you think Jesus could walk on water?

JESUS, NO ONE ELSE CAN WALK ON WATER. YOU ARE TRULY SPECIAL. AMEN.

# God talks to Jesus

Jesus took Peter, James, and John up a mountain to pray. Jesus grew brighter and brighter until even his clothes shone dazzling white. The friends were amazed. They saw Moses and Elijah, two of God's prophets from long ago, talking with Jesus!

Should we wait to see a miracle like this before we listen to Jesus?

Suddenly a misty cloud came down, and they heard God say, "This is my Son. Listen to him!"

DEAR GOD, PLEASE HELP ME TO LISTEN TO JESUS. AMEN.

# The kind stranger

Jesus told another story: A man was lying badly hurt by the side of the road. A priest came along. But he did not help, he just walked away!

Then another important man walked by. But he did not stop to help either.

At last, a kind stranger stopped. He bandaged the man, took him to an inn, and looked after him there. "Be kind like the stranger in this story," said Jesus.

How was the stranger a better person than the important man?

PLEASE, GOD, HELP ME TO BE KIND TO OTHERS. AMEN.

# A prayer to God

"Jesus, teach us how to talk to God," his friends asked. So Jesus taught them this prayer:

THANK YOU, DEAR GOD, FOR LISTENING TO OUR PRAYERS. AMEN.

Our Father in heaven, may everyone know and love you. Come and be our King.

Give us today the food we need. Forgive the bad things we do. Help us to forgive others, too.

When we want to do something bad, help us choose to do good instead.

Do you ever say a prayer like this one?

# The lost sheep

Everyone crowded around as Jesus told this story about what God's kingdom is like:

There was once a shepherd who had one hundred sheep. One day he discovered one was missing.

DEAR GOD, THANK YOU FOR HELPING THE SHEPHERD FIND HIS SHEEP. AMEN.

He searched up and down, near and far. Finally he found it. He was so happy that he carried it all the way home! "I've found my lost sheep!" he called to his friends. "Let's have a party!"

Why is this story good news for us when we make mistakes?

Like the shepherd in the story, God is happy when even one sinner turns back to him.

How is this story like the story of the lost sheep?

# Coming home

There was once a son who left home. He soon spent his father's money.

"I'm hungry and unhappy," the young man thought. "I'll go back and tell my father I'm sorry."

As soon as his father saw him, he ran to hug him. "My son has come home!" he called to his servants. "Let's have a party!"

"God is so happy when we come home to him," Jesus said.

GOD, THANK YOU FOR LOVING US EVEN WHEN WE MAKE MISTAKES. AMEN.

# Jesus gives new life

Martha and Mary were very sad because
their brother Lazarus had died.

"I can give new life," Jesus said to them.
"Anyone who trusts me will never really die."

He went to the place where Lazarus was buried.
"Move the stone away!" Jesus ordered.
"Lazarus, come out!" he called.

And to everyone's amazement, Lazarus walked out alive and well.

Why do you think Jesus brought Lazarus back to life?

JESUS, YOU ARE GOOD AND POWERFUL. YOU HAVE DONE MANY WONDERFUL THINGS. AMEN.

# Jesus and the children

Some people brought their children to see Jesus. Jesus' friends said, "Go away! Don't bother Jesus. He's much too busy." Jesus was angry with them.

DEAR GOD, THANK YOU FOR ALWAYS TAKING CARE OF ME. AMEN.

"Let the children come to me," he said. "Don't stop them. God wants children in his kingdom."
The children ran to Jesus' open arms.
He hugged them and asked God
to take special care of them.

If you were a child back then, would you have wanted to see Jesus?

# Expensive perfume

As Jesus and his friends were eating, Mary poured
her precious bottle of perfume over Jesus' feet.
Then she wiped them gently with her long hair.
A wonderful, sweet smell filled the room.

"Mary should have sold that perfume and given the money to the poor," complained Judas. But Jesus was pleased with Mary. "Mary has done something very special for me," he said.

How did Mary honor Jesus?

DEAR GOD, THANK YOU FOR EVERYTHING THAT YOU DO. AMEN.

# Entering Jerusalem

Jesus rode into Jerusalem on a young donkey.
The people spread branches and cloaks
on the ground—like a carpet for a king.

On what day each year do we remember this event?

The crowds waved branches to welcome Jesus.
"Hooray for God's special king!" they cheered.
"Who is this man?" people asked.
"It's Jesus! God's messenger!"
the crowds replied.

DEAR GOD, I WOULD LIKE TO SAY
THANK YOU FOR JESUS. AMEN.

# Jesus is angry

God's temple was busy when Jesus arrived.

"Buy a lamb here," shouted some sellers.
"Doves for sale!" yelled others.

Jesus was very angry. There was so
much noise; no one could talk to God.

"God's house is a special place to pray," said
Jesus, pushing over a stall piled high with money,
"not somewhere to buy and sell and cheat!"
Then he chased them all out of the temple.

# Washing feet

One evening, during supper, Jesus got up, tied a towel around his waist, and began to wash his friends' feet. They were shocked— it was the servant's job to wash feet.

DEAR GOD, PLEASE HELP ME TO BE LOVING AND HELPFUL LIKE JESUS. AMEN.

"Jesus, you mustn't wash our feet," said Peter. "I'm washing your feet because I love you," said Jesus. "Now copy me. Love and help each other."

Why did Jesus choose to do a servant's job?

# A special meal

Jesus was eating a special meal with his friends when he took some bread, thanked God, broke it in pieces, and handed it around.

"This is my body," he said. "I give it for you." Then he took a cup of wine, thanked God, and passed it around. "Drink this," he said. "I will die for many people because God has promised to forgive them."

Like Jesus, do you ever thank God before eating a meal?

THANK YOU, JESUS, FOR GIVING YOUR LIFE FOR EVERYONE. AMEN.

# Jesus is taken prisoner

Jesus was praying in the garden.
He was sad because he knew
he was going to die soon.

How did Jesus
show bravery and
loyalty to God in
his prayers?

"Father, don't let me die," he prayed.
"But if dying is part of your plan then
I will do what you want."

Suddenly Jesus' friend Judas arrived, leading a crowd of Jesus' enemies. He kissed Jesus. At once the soldiers surrounded Jesus and took him prisoner.

DEAR GOD, THANK YOU FOR LISTENING TO ME WHEN I FEEL SAD OR AFRAID. AMEN.

# Peter lets Jesus down

Could you own up to knowing Jesus if it might get you hurt?

Peter followed Jesus and the soldiers.
"Aren't you Jesus' friend?" asked a servant girl.
Peter shook his head, "No! I don't know him!"

DEAR GOD, PLEASE HELP ME WHEN IT'S
HARD TO BE YOUR FRIEND. AMEN.

Two more people
asked if he knew Jesus.
"No!" said Peter. "No!"

Suddenly a rooster crowed. Peter remembered
that Jesus had said: "Before the rooster
crows, you will say three times that you're
not my friend." Peter burst into tears.

# Jesus is left to die

Jesus' enemies took Jesus to Pilate, the Roman ruler. Pilate asked Jesus lots of questions. Then he said, "Jesus has not done anything wrong. I will let him go." "NO!" the people shouted. "Kill Jesus! Nail him to a cross!"

JESUS, THANK YOU FOR LOVING EVERYONE ENOUGH TO DIE TO SAVE THEM. AMEN.

So Pilate's soldiers nailed Jesus to a cross and left him to die.

How do you think Jesus' family and friends felt when he died?

Jesus knew that he had done what God wanted. "My work is finished!" he cried. Then he died.

# A sad day

Jesus was dead. Nicodemus and Joseph of Arimathea had been afraid to say they were Jesus' friends.

DEAR GOD, THANK YOU FOR BEING THERE WHEN I AM SAD. AMEN.

But now they showed that they loved him. They wrapped Jesus' body in cloth with precious perfumes and carefully put him in a new tomb.

How did Jesus' friends honor him after he died?

Together they rolled the heavy stone across the doorway. Then they walked sadly away.

# Jesus is alive!

Two days later Mary Magdalene stood outside Jesus' tomb. It was empty! Jesus' body was gone.

Why do you think Mary didn't recognize Jesus?

"Why are you crying?" asked a man standing nearby. "Have you taken Jesus away?" Mary sobbed.

"Mary!" said the man gently. Mary looked up.
It was Jesus! He smiled. "Go and tell my friends."
Mary ran all the way. She couldn't wait to
tell them the good news—Jesus was ALIVE!

THANK YOU, GOD, FOR EASTER TIME. IT'S
WONDERFUL THAT JESUS IS ALIVE! AMEN.

# A surprise

Two of Jesus' friends met a man on their way home.

Do you think Jesus' friends believed Mary?

"Jesus was killed three days ago," they told him, "but Mary says Jesus is alive again!"

"God promised this would happen to his special king," said the stranger. At supper time, the man thanked God for the bread, then gave it to the friends. Suddenly the friends knew— the stranger was Jesus. He really was alive!

DEAR GOD, HELP ME TO KNOW EVERY DAY THAT JESUS IS ALIVE. AMEN.

# Tell everyone!

The two friends ran back to Jerusalem.
"We've seen Jesus!" they said to all of Jesus' friends.

Suddenly Jesus was there, too!
Everyone stopped talking.
"Don't be scared," Jesus said.
"It's me. Touch me—I'm not a ghost!"

They were so happy to see Jesus alive again. "Tell everyone everywhere about me," Jesus told them. "Because of me, they can be God's friends again."

Why were Jesus' friends scared when they saw him?

THANK YOU, JESUS. IT'S GREAT THAT I CAN BE GOD'S FRIEND. AMEN.

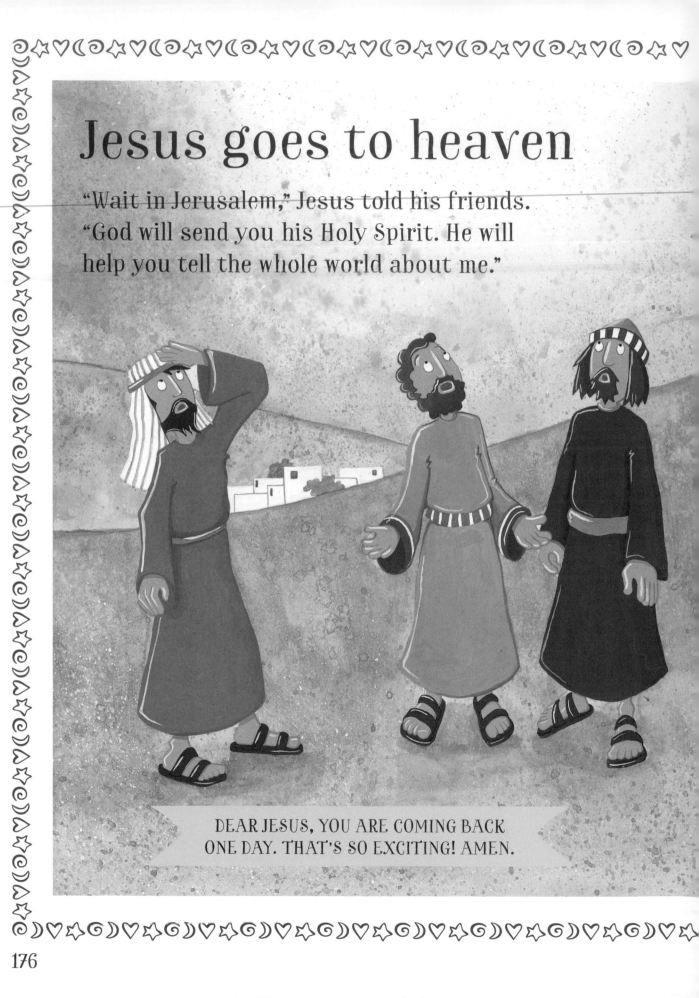

# Jesus goes to heaven

"Wait in Jerusalem," Jesus told his friends.
"God will send you his Holy Spirit. He will
help you tell the whole world about me."

DEAR JESUS, YOU ARE COMING BACK
ONE DAY. THAT'S SO EXCITING! AMEN.

Then, before their eyes, Jesus was taken up to heaven.

Suddenly two men dressed in white appeared.

Who do you think the men in white might have been?

"Why are you standing here looking at the sky?" they asked. "Jesus will come back one day."

# The Holy Spirit

Jesus' friends were praying when...
whoosh! A sound like a rushing wind
roared through the house.

A flickering flame rested gently on
each head. God's Holy Spirit had come
to help them tell others about Jesus.

When the people from other countries heard what God had done, they wanted to be Jesus' friends, too.

What do we call people who are Jesus' friends today?

THANK YOU, GOD, FOR SENDING YOUR HOLY SPIRIT. AMEN.

# Jesus speaks to Paul

Paul did not believe that Jesus was God's special king. He hated Jesus' friends.

He set off to find them and put them in prison. FLASH! A bright light shone. Paul fell to the ground. "Paul, why do you hate me and hurt me?" said a voice.

"Who are you?" asked Paul.
"I am Jesus!"

Paul was shocked. Jesus was alive!
From that moment Paul became Jesus' friend.
"Go and tell everyone about me," Jesus said.

How did Jesus get Paul to help spread his messages?

DEAR GOD, THANK YOU FOR YOUR POWER
TO MAKE PEOPLE WELL. AMEN.

# Friends of Jesus

Paul traveled to many places telling people about Jesus. One night a man called to Paul in a dream, "Come to Macedonia! Help us!"

How did Paul help spread Jesus' message?

The next day Paul sailed to Macedonia.

THANK YOU, GOD, FOR ALL THE PEOPLE
WHO TELL ME ABOUT JESUS. AMEN.

There he met Lydia, a rich woman, and her
friends. He told them about Jesus. So Lydia
and her friends became friends of Jesus, too.

# Paul is taken prisoner

One day, when Paul was at the temple,
Jesus' enemies tried to kill him.
"Paul tells lies!" they shouted.

Just then the Roman commander
marched in. His soldiers stopped
the people from hurting Paul.

Paul explained that God wanted everyone to know Jesus was alive, but the crowd shouted, "NO! Get rid of Paul."
So the commander put Paul in prison.

# God keeps his promise

"The Roman emperor must decide if I am right," Paul said.

So the soldiers took Paul and set sail for Rome. Before long the ship was caught in a raging storm.

"Don't be afraid," said Paul. "God will keep us all safe."

How did Paul show his trust in God?

As the ship broke up, everyone swam for the shore. At last they reached the land—cold, wet, but safe.

God had kept his promise.

THANK YOU, GOD. YOU ALWAYS KEEP YOUR PROMISES! AMEN.

# Letters from Paul

Finally Paul and the soldiers arrived in Rome.

Paul was still a prisoner, but he was allowed to write to all the people he had met on his travels. They had become friends of Jesus, too.

They told Paul their problems and he wrote back to help them. "Keep on loving Jesus," Paul wrote, "and keep on loving each other."

Would you want to help others if you were in prison?

THANK YOU, DEAR GOD, FOR MY FRIENDS. AMEN.

# A new heaven and earth

DEAR GOD, THANK YOU FOR HEAVEN
AND EARTH. AMEN.

Would you like to live in the new earth? Why?

One day John saw a man—strong, good, and shining bright. It was Jesus!

"Write to my friends," Jesus said. "Tell them that God is going to make a new heaven and a new earth where no one will be hurt or die! All God's friends will live with him forever."

# Index

This index shows where to find some favorite Bible stories in this book and also shows groups of stories that link together.